W9-BDN-684

1875

920
STO

Stone, Melissa

Clouds of war

$13.96

Clouds of War

Program Consultants

Stephanie Abraham Hirsh, Ph.D.
Associate Director
National Staff Development Council
Dallas, Texas

Louise Matteoni, Ph.D.
Professor of Education
Brooklyn College
City University of New York

Karen Tindel Wiggins
Social Studies Consultant
Richardson Independent School District
Richardson, Texas

Renee Levitt
Educational Consultant
Scarsdale, New York

Steck-Vaughn Company

A Subsidiary of National Education Corporation

Clouds of War

BY
Melissa Stone

Steck-Vaughn Literature Library
Moments in American History

RISKING IT ALL
REBELLION'S SONG
CREATIVE DAYS
RACING TO THE WEST
YOU DON'T OWN ME!
CLOUDS OF WAR
A CRY FOR ACTION
LARGER THAN LIFE
FLYING HIGH
BRIGHTER TOMORROWS

Illustrations: D.J. Simison: pp. 8-9, 10, 12, 15, 17, 19; Christa Kieffer: pp. 20-21, 22, 25, 27, 28-29, 31; Ron Himler: cover art, pp. 32-33, 35, 36, 39, 40-41, 43; Fredrick Porter: pp. 44-45, 47, 49, 50-51, 53, 55; Al Fiorentino: pp. 56-57, 58, 61, 62, 65, 67; Lyle Miller: 68-69, 70, 73, 74, 76, 79.

Project Editor: Anne Souby

Design: Kirchoff/Wohlberg, Inc.

ISBN 0-8114-4080-X (pbk.)
ISBN 0-8114-2670-X (lib. bdg.)   LC 89-110893

CONTENTS

1860

◄ **JULIA WARD HOWE**
As the Civil War raged, she was moved to write a song that still marches on. (1861-1862)

ROBERT SMALLS ►
Forced to serve in the Confederate Navy, a slave plans a daring escape and sails to freedom. (1862)

◄ **STONEWALL JACKSON**
Outnumbered two to one, this Southern general marched his troops deep into enemy ranks for a surprise attack. (1863)

◄ **PHILIP SHERIDAN**
His path of destruction
through the Shenandoah
Valley meant the end for
the South.
(1864)

MORRIS FOOTE ►
No Confederate prison could
hold him in his determination
to rejoin the Union army.
(1864)

◄ **JOHN WILKES BOOTH**
One idea obsessed him—
to kill the President
of the United States.
(1865)

JULIA WARD HOWE

"THE BATTLE HYMN OF THE REPUBLIC"

When I look around, I see everyone giving something to the war effort. The soldiers are fighting. Many women are working as nurses. My own husband is helping with medical supplies. I wish I could do something to help. If only I could find a way …

QUICK!" shouted a Union soldier. "Everyone has to move out. The Confederates are headed this way!"

Julia Ward Howe scanned the Virginia field frantically.

"How can this be?" she gasped. "I thought the North controlled this area."

"Not anymore," called the soldier. "The Confederates are moving up from the south, and it looks like there's going to be a battle. The colonel has ordered some troops to head them off. You civilians had better hurry back to Washington!"

Julia and her husband, Dr. Samuel Howe, raced to their carriage. They had come to the countryside this day in 1861 to see some of the Union troops and enjoy a picnic with other relief workers. Suddenly, however, their calm day in the country was turning into a nightmare. No one had expected the Civil War to threaten the capital.

As they rushed back toward Washington, the 42-year-old Howe was overcome with fear. This was the first time she had been near any battles. The Civil War had been raging for seven months, but she lived in Massachusetts, far away from the fighting. She hadn't realized that her trip to Washington would put her quite so close to the combat.

"This war is so terrible. I hope it will end soon," she thought as the carriage bounced along.

Then, in the distance, she heard the bugles signaling a Union retreat. Suddenly, the carriage was engulfed by retreating Northern soldiers. Everyone was rushing back to the safety of Washington, D.C. The number of fleeing soldiers and the confusion made travel difficult.

The people in Julia Howe's party became more tense and frightened. Howe, too, felt her heart thumping wildly.

"Do you think we will make it safely?" one man asked.

"How long before we reach Washington?" called a woman.

"Can't this carriage move any faster?" cried someone else.

Julia Howe knew that panic would not help. They would have to sit quietly and endure the long, slow ride back. To boost her own spirits and those of her companions, she began to sing a familiar tune.

"John Brown's body lies a-moldering in the grave," she sang out.

Others joined in for the chorus.

> Glory, glory, hallelujah!
> Glory, glory, hallelujah!
> Glory, glory, hallelujah!
>   His soul goes marching on!

Groups of soldiers joined the singing.

"Good for you, ma'am," one soldier yelled out to Howe. She smiled and thought that she had always loved the tune of the old folk song. When she was a little girl, the song had different lyrics. It was called, "Say Brothers, Will We Meet You Over on the Other Shore?" Lately, however, the

lyrics about John Brown had become popular. John Brown had been killed for trying to free the slaves. He had become a Northern hero and had been immortalized in song.

"You know, Julia," said one of the women in her carriage, "you're a gifted poet. You should write some different words for that tune. Something grand and stirring."

Julia Howe gave a little laugh. "I have often wanted to," she said. "But writing is such a chore for me. It often takes me days just to find the right words for a single line. I'm sure I could never write a better version of the song."

Finally, the carriage crossed the bridge over the Potomac River and arrived in Washington. Exhausted, Mrs. Howe and her husband returned to their room at the Willard Hotel. After an early supper, they retired for the night.

A few hours later, in the middle of the night, Howe woke up. She lay in bed listening to the sounds outside her window. On the street below, she heard soldiers marching by. Their feet marked out a steady beat on the cobblestones. In the darkened room, she could picture the grim faces of the soldiers as they marched bravely off to battle. The memory of the fear she had experienced earlier in the day overcame her.

Then, slowly, Howe became aware of something else. Words were swimming around in her head. They were not just any words; they were new words for the song she had sung that day. The poem flowed freely into her mind, in perfect rhythm, in perfect form. Excitedly she jumped out of bed and groped her way to the desk where a paper and pen lay waiting. Her pen flew across the page as she tried to capture the song. She did not bother to light a lamp. She wrote blindly, afraid to stop for fear of losing the inspiration.

> Mine eyes have seen the glory of the coming of
>   the Lord:
> He is trampling out the vintage where the grapes
>   of wrath are stored;
> He hath loosed the fateful lightning of his ter-
>   rible swift sword:
>   His truth is marching on.

Line by line, the song tumbled onto the paper. As she wrote the last words, Howe felt a sense of satisfaction and completion. She crept back to bed and drifted off to sleep.

W HEN she awoke the next morning, Howe remembered the events of the night and the new song she had composed. But she could not recall any of the words.

"Thank goodness I wrote them down. I only hope I can read the words," she thought.

Jumping up, she found the paper she had used to scrawl down the lines. Her handwriting was sloppy and shaky, but with effort she could read all the words.

"Yes," she murmured. "This is good. It is right. After all, the North isn't just fighting for control of the South. We're fighting for truth, for freedom, and for the abolition of all slavery."

Howe submitted her poem to *Atlantic Monthly* magazine, and it was published in February 1862 as "The Battle Hymn of the Republic." She was proud of the special words that had been inspired by her trip to Washington.

AT first no one paid much attention to the song. The country's eyes were focused on the grim realities of the war. One man, however, took time to study the lyrics carefully. An army chaplain named Charles McCabe read the words again and again. They seemed to penetrate into his very soul. As he repeated them, he thought, "That's one song I want to remember."

Several months later, Confederate troops attacked Winchester, Virginia. Charles McCabe and other Union soldiers were captured and placed in Libby Prison in Richmond, Virginia.

Conditions at Libby Prison were dreadful. The prisoners were kept in one large, hot, windowless room. There were no chairs, no beds, no clean clothes. Day after day McCabe and the others sat helplessly on the floor of the prison cell. McCabe secretly hoped he might be released in a prisoner exchange. He also prayed for some news of Union triumphs.

One night a Confederate jailer appeared in the doorway of the cell.

"Great news!" he announced in a boisterous voice. "We just heard there's been a major battle in Pennsylvania. The Confederates have scored a huge victory!"

This news left McCabe and his cellmates desolate. A blanket of hopelessness dropped over them.

A little while later, a slave named Ben slipped into the room. Ben came every night with a small cart of food for the hungry prisoners to share. This night, however, he brought something better than food. He brought good news.

"I just heard 'em talking outside," he told the prisoners. "There *was* a major battle. It was at some place called Gettysburg. But they lied to you—the Confederates didn't win. The North did!"

Suddenly the prison cell erupted with wild celebration. The prisoners cheered, cried, and hugged each other joyously. Charles McCabe jumped to his feet. The song that he had read several months before flashed through his head. In a grand baritone voice, he began to sing it.

As his voice floated above the cheers, the prisoners quieted to listen. One by one, they joined in for the choruses. Soon all the men were singing "Glory, glory, hallelujah."

Then McCabe came to the final verse. With tears streaming down his face, he sang out the words that had so impressed him.

By the time he had finished singing, many of the prisoners also had tears running down their cheeks. The song traveled directly into their hearts. Although it had been written by a woman who was neither a soldier nor a prisoner, the special words beautifully expressed the hopes, beliefs, and determination of every person in the cell. The prisoners knew what a sacrifice each had made to the struggle to preserve the Union and win freedom for all. But they knew that they were not alone in the fight. And after hearing the song, they knew that the cause was worth any sacrifice.

J ULIA Ward Howe was nowhere near Libby Prison that July night. But later she learned what had taken place. When Charles McCabe was released in a prisoner exchange, he spread the story of his experience across the North. Those who heard his story were touched by the image of the lonely prisoners singing a song of freedom and courage. Union troops everywhere learned the words. The song buoyed the spirits of countless young soldiers.

Julia Ward Howe's song became a powerful symbol for the Union. To many people, the song represented the battle for the preservation of the Union and the right of all people to be free.

ROBERT SMALLS
SAILING FOR THE UNION

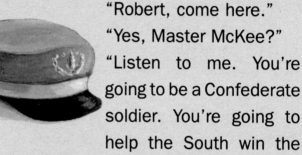

"Robert, come here."

"Yes, Master McKee?"

"Listen to me. You're going to be a Confederate soldier. You're going to help the South win the war. I've signed you up! I felt it my duty as a Southerner to loan you to the Navy for a while. Since you're a good pilot and know the Charleston Harbor so well, the Confederate Navy will be happy to have you. You start tomorrow on the transport ship *Planter.*"

R OBERT Smalls stared numbly at his master. He couldn't believe what he had just heard. Finally, he turned and walked slowly toward home, clenching and unclenching his fists.

"Imagine me fighting for the Confederacy!" he snarled. "Fighting alongside slaveowners! Fighting to keep my people in chains! I think I'd rather die. And what about Hannah and the children?" He knew it was useless to protest to his master. Slaves had no rights.

The next morning, he reluctantly reported for duty on the *Planter*, a Confederate ship.

For more than six months, Smalls worked on the 150-foot steamship. He learned how to use the 32-pound pivot gun and the 24-pound howitzer mounted on the deck. He learned to run the

boiler. He learned how to chart the course and steer the boat through the surging coastal tides. He became friends with the seven other slaves who manned the *Planter*. He even learned to get along with the three white men who were the officers — the captain, mate, and engineer.

Still, Smalls hated being there. He knew he was helping the Confederate cause, and he detested doing it. Every day his resentment grew. Slowly a plan began to take shape in his mind. He knew he would have to wait for the right opportunity. On the night of May 12, 1862, Robert Smalls knew his chance had arrived. He could put his daring plan into action.

On that night, the three white officers left the steamer to go ashore.

"Robert," said the captain, "we've got some business in town. We'll be gone for a few hours. Take care of the *Planter* until we get back."

"Yes, sir," said Smalls obediently.

As soon as the officers were out of sight, he gathered the black crewmen together.

"Listen," he said, "I have been waiting for this moment. It is our big chance. With some cooperation and a little luck, we can get out of here."

"What do you mean?" asked Benjamin, the stoker.

"I mean we can escape," Smalls said in a hushed voice. "We can sail this ship right out of the harbor into free waters."

"But where will we go?" asked crewman Stubb.

"We'll go out to the Union ships in the Atlantic Ocean. They are blockading the coast. Then we'll surrender and join them."

"But that means — if we do that, we'll be — " Benjamin stumbled over his words.

"If we do it, we'll be free," Smalls said, finishing the thought for him.

A wave of excitement swept over the group.

"Go home and get your families," Smalls ordered them. "Then come back here as fast as you can. We'll talk about the details when you return."

The men scrambled off the *Planter* and ran to get their wives and children.

WHILE they were gone, Smalls paced the deck nervously. He knew his plan held many risks. The runaway ship would have to sail past several Confederate checkpoints. Smalls shivered at the danger involved in the escape.

"We just have to make the Confederate guards think we're on a routine run," he told himself.

He knew that if the plan failed, his life was over. He and the other runaways would be killed.

By 2:00 A.M., the seven crew members had returned with their families. Benjamin had brought Robert's wife Hannah and their two children. As Hannah boarded, she looked at her husband with pride and fear in her eyes. Smalls gave her a reassuring hug, then called the group together.

"Listen," he said in a somber voice. "You need to think very carefully about this. Remember, if you come with me, you are risking death. This is a dangerous plan. Many things can go wrong. The Confederates may get suspicious when they see us sailing at such an early hour. They may try to stop us and question us. If that happens, I'm going to ignite the gunpowder in the hatch."

"But that will kill us all!" cried Stubb.

"That's right," said Smalls grimly. "But considering what they would do to us, I think that's better than letting them take us alive."

A heavy silence settled over the group. They all knew he was right. After a moment, Smalls spoke again.

"If any of you think the risk is too great, speak up now. You're free to leave and go back home. No one will blame you. It's now or never. Once I fire up the boiler and we start moving, there can be no turning back."

For a few moments uncertainty hung in the air. Smalls held his breath. He prayed that his crew would stay with him. He needed their help. He knew he could never get the steamer out of the harbor alone.

"Count me in," said Stubb at last. The other crew members murmured their agreement also.

"All right," said Smalls excitedly. "Then let's get going."

He turned to Hannah. "Take the women and children down below," he told her. "Make sure the children stay quiet. One sound could alert the guards and ruin our chances."

Hannah nodded. She motioned to the other women and children to follow her.

Next Smalls sent Stubb to light the kindling and

start the fire under the boiler. He ordered Benjamin to untie the ropes that moored the *Planter* to the dock. He asked all the other crew members to take their usual work places on deck. Then he himself walked back to the captain's cabin and broke the lock. He grabbed the captain's hat and went to the pilothouse.

A S the *Planter* headed out, Smalls blew the whistle to alert the shore sentinel that the ship was leaving.

"Why are you doing that?" hissed Benjamin in alarm.

"We have to do everything exactly the way we would normally. If not, they'll catch on to us for sure. Our best hope is for them to think the *Planter* is heading out for an ordinary transport assignment."

"If you say so," said Benjamin, but he still looked concerned.

As they pulled away from the wharf, a crewman raised the Confederate flag and the South Carolina Palmetto flag. Smalls steered the ship through the harbor. He was tempted to open up the boiler and run the steamer at full speed. But he knew that such haste would create suspicion. He forced himself to keep the *Planter* cruising along at its usual pace.

When they neared the first checkpoint, Smalls put on the captain's hat. He pulled the hat down low on his head and struck a pose that he had seen the captain strike many times. He swallowed hard, took a deep breath, and tried to remain calm.

"This is it," he thought to himself. "Our first real test. I hope all goes well."

When the ship pulled alongside the Confederate guards on shore, Smalls blew the whistle and gave the proper salute. The guards waved back, motioning the *Planter* to continue its course.

"We did it! We passed the first test!" thought Smalls joyously, but he knew it was much too early to celebrate. Several other checkpoints still loomed in the distance.

ONE by one, the *Planter* passed them. Finally only one remained — Fort Sumter. Smalls knew that it would be the most difficult to get past. As the last checkpoint before open waters, it watched outgoing ships very carefully.

Smalls thought of Hannah down below. She was doing a wonderful job keeping everyone quiet. He knew it was no easy task — surely the children were terrified to find themselves in the hull of a strange ship in the middle of the night.

"Well," he thought, "one way or the other, their fears will soon be ended."

The *Planter* pulled alongside Fort Sumter, and Smalls gave the secret signal — three sharp blows on the whistle, followed by a long, slow, hissing one. Still wearing the captain's hat, he watched as the sentinel called to the corporal of the guard. A minute passed. Smalls began to panic. Why hadn't they given the signal for the *Planter* to pass? Had they sensed something wrong?

Smalls felt as though his heart would burst. He glanced down at the hatch where the gunpowder was stored. Would he have to ignite it? Slowly he reached for a match. But at that very moment, a whistle blew at Fort Sumter. It was the signal he was waiting for. It was just one short blast — but it signaled the *Planter* to continue on its course to the sea.

WITH a sigh of relief, Smalls steered the steamer out into the open water. When it was out of reach of the Confederate guns, he gave a loud shout.

"Lower that Confederate flag! Lower the Palmetto! Put up the white flag of surrender. Tell everyone below deck that we are safe! We are free! We are in Union waters!"

Within minutes, the *Planter* drew up alongside the Union ship *Onward*. As Union guards boarded the ship, Smalls explained what he had done. Instantly the crew of the *Onward* welcomed Smalls, his crewmen, and their families into the ranks of the Union.

"Where did you find the courage for such a bold escape?" asked one Union soldier admiringly.

"I just wanted all of us to be free," Smalls whispered as he hugged his wife and children.

Thomas J. Jackson

The South's Stone Wall

Don't give up the fight! Keep pressing! Show those Northerners who we are! Keep fighting! Look yonder! There's Jackson standing like a stone wall. His troops can't be budged by the enemy. Be like them! Anchor yourselves! Don't fall back! Make the Battle of Bull Run a victory for the South! Stand strong like Stonewall Jackson!

THOMAS "Stonewall" Jackson broke out into a broad grin when he saw the train approaching. As soon as it came to a stop, he dashed up the steps and into his wife's compartment.

"Anna! Sweetheart!" he cried joyously. "How are you? I've missed you so much! This must be Julia. What a beautiful baby daughter we have."

It was April 20, 1863, and Stonewall Jackson had not seen his wife in thirteen months. He had never seen his daughter, Julia, who was now four months old. Anna and the baby had stayed at home in Charlotte, North Carolina, while Jackson had been traveling with the Confederate army. He served as general and advisor to Robert E. Lee, commander of Virginia's Confederate troops.

Jackson hurried his family to a farmhouse near his headquarters in Fredericksburg, Virginia. They spent the next nine days in a happy reunion.

"Anna," he said one lovely morning, "won't it be wonderful when the war is over and we can be a family again?"

"Yes," she said wistfully. "I think of little else."

Suddenly, an excited Confederate messenger burst through the front door of the farmhouse.

"General Jackson, sir!" the messenger cried, panting, "Union soldiers are headed this way! Over 130,000 of them! You must hurry, sir —

General Lee wants you to report to headquarters immediately."

Instantly Jackson felt his pulse quicken. His face took on a hard, stern look. The reality of the war was returning.

"It must be 'Fighting Joe' Hooker's troops," he said quietly. Then turning to Anna, he said, "You must go now. It's dangerous to remain here. Take Julia and get on the first train headed south. You must get home safely. I don't know what I would do if anything ever happened to you or to Julia."

As Anna bundled up the baby, Jackson walked over and gave them each a quick kiss.

"Take care of yourself," he whispered to his beloved wife.

"You, too," she murmured.

Then Stonewall Jackson dashed outside and galloped off to headquarters. When he arrived, General Lee told him about the enemy's troop movements.

"'Fighting Joe' Hooker is crossing the Rappahannock River and closing in on Chancellorsville, just a few miles northwest of here. When his men reach Chancellorsville, I suspect Hooker will launch a full-scale attack and try to surround us. If we let him do that, he'll destroy our army, and the South might lose the war."

Jackson nodded thoughtfully. "You're right," he said slowly, "but how can we stop him? We're outnumbered two to one."

"With 60,000 men up against 130,000, our only chance is to stage a surprise attack," declared General Lee boldly. "We shall meet Hooker at Chancellorsville and drive him back across the

river." General Lee paused. "Well, Stonewall, do you think it can be done?"

Jackson did not respond immediately. His mind was racing, imagining all the things that could go wrong with such an attack. Yet, he knew that a desperate move was needed. He could think of no other way to head off Hooker's troops. He cleared his throat and gave his reply.

"Yes, sir," he said. "Yes, I think it can be done."

SO, early on May 1, with Jackson at his side, General Lee gave the command. About 15,000 troops would stay in Fredericksburg to prevent a rear attack by Union soldiers. The remaining 45,000 would follow Generals Lee and Jackson to Chancellorsville.

The journey did not take long. By midday, the Confederates arrived on the outskirts of Chancellorsville. General Lee ordered his men to halt.

The two generals walked to a clearing in the woods. Here, away from the noise and tension of the troops, Lee and Jackson could talk openly.

"A head-on attack would be suicide," Jackson stated flatly.

"I'm afraid you're right," agreed General Lee grimly. "The enemy far outnumbers us. But if we went around and attacked from the side, perhaps we could catch them off guard."

Jackson hardly knew what to say. General Lee's plan meant creeping past the front lines, past thousands of Union soldiers, deep into enemy territory. It was a frightening idea. But it was also brilliant. The Union troops would never expect such a brash move from the Confederate forces.

"I think we should try it, sir," said Jackson. "Just give me the order and I'll swing my troops over to Hooker's right flank."

"You have your orders. Move out when you're ready. Good luck, Stonewall. Good luck, my friend," replied Lee.

"Thank you, sir," said Jackson, and he gave General Lee a quick salute. "I will head out early tomorrow morning with about 25,000 troops. That will leave you enough men to distract Hooker and keep him busy until my men get into position."

BEFORE dawn the next morning, Jackson roused his troops and ordered them to prepare to march. He told only his top aides about his plan.

"A flank attack to Hooker's right?" cried General Rhodes. "It'll never work!"

"It must work," said Jackson curtly. "Don't tell your men what we're planning to do. I'm afraid they might panic, and then all will be lost."

"We've got fifteen miles to cover," Jackson continued, "and every inch of it is through enemy territory. We will march single file and pray that Hooker doesn't see us."

Trying to appear calm and confident, the officers got their men in line. Then, with Jackson leading the way, the troops set off on the dangerous march. The column was six miles long.

All morning they moved one by one through the woods. Then Jackson saw that the trail suddenly opened onto a wide field.

"Quickly!" Jackson urged in a loud whisper. "Cut over to the left. Avoid the field!"

A T 3:00 that afternoon, Jackson came within sight of the Union camp.

"What now, sir?" asked General Rhodes.

"Now," said Jackson quietly, "we wait for all our men to get into position."

It took two hours to move all the men into the proper columns. They had to move slowly and carefully. They were so close to the enemy that any wrong move or loud noise would give them away. At last, everyone was ready.

Stonewall Jackson took one last look around at the beautiful trees. A religious man, he said a silent prayer. Then he pushed all doubts and fears out of his mind. With his jaw set, and the stance that earned him the nickname "Stonewall," he gave the order.

"Sound the charge," he said. "We are pressing forward."

The sharp blast of bugles filled the air. Jackson and his men leaped through the underbrush toward the Union troops. Bursting into the camp,

they found the Union troops cooking supper. Terrified, the Northern soldiers scrambled to flee. But the Confederates pounced on them before they could get away. Fierce fighting broke out, and the crack of musket shots drowned out all other sounds.

By 6:00 P.M., Jackson's men had completely destroyed Hooker's right flank. Union soldiers were running frantically through the forest, trying to escape the bloody attack.

"We've cut Hooker's right line to pieces," General Rhodes shouted excitedly. "The enemy is retreating. This is one of the most stunning victories ever!"

JACKSON'S men were eager to rest. But Jackson wasn't satisfied. He wanted to push farther into Chancellorsville and crush Hooker's entire army.

"I'm going to ride ahead and find a new trail for us to follow," he announced. "Tomorrow we must continue our pursuit of the enemy." Then he rode off into the night. A few of his men followed him, hoping to change his mind.

"General Jackson," one man called in a loud whisper. "General Jackson, you might stumble into a pocket of enemy troops! You might be captured or even killed. Shouldn't you send someone else to scout?"

"I've got to see for myself," Jackson replied, and kept riding.

After finding a trail, he rode back toward his own troops. As he neared his men, he could just make out their shapes in the moonlight. But when they looked in his direction, all they could see was a shadowy, ominous form.

"It's the enemy!" cried one soldier.

"Fire!" cried a Confederate officer. "Fire and repeat fire!"

Before Jackson knew what was happening, musket fire from his own soldiers ripped into his left arm and shoulder.

When his men realized what they had done, they were horrified. Quickly they rushed him to a doctor, who bandaged his wounds and sent him off to a field hospital.

At first, his wounds healed well. But then pneumonia set in. Jackson was growing weaker. The doctor sent a message to his wife on May 7. By the time Anna and the baby got to the hospital, Jackson was fading in and out of consciousness. But when he saw his beloved wife, he gathered his strength and spoke.

"My darling," he said, "I love you very much."

On the afternoon of May 10, 1863, Thomas "Stonewall" Jackson died. The South did win the Battle of Chancellorsville. But in doing so, it lost one of its greatest generals.

MORRIS FOOTE
A DARING ESCAPE

It seems so long ago ... seven months ago I was captured by the Confederates. Ever since then, I've been rotting in this prison camp in Columbia, South Carolina. Conditions are dreadful. Nothing to sleep on but pine branches, nothing to eat but dry bread or mush. Guns pointing at me day and night. No way to help the North win the war. Unless ... I escape!

ORRIS Foote lingered near the prisoners' food table on the morning of November 29, 1864. Slyly he reached out and grabbed an extra piece of cornbread. He quickly slipped it into the pocket of his pants. Then he glanced over at the guards to make sure they hadn't noticed.

"Lucky for me these guards are just young country boys," he thought grimly.

Later Foote huddled in a corner of the prison yard with his friend and fellow inmate, Bob Coates. Morris took out the stolen cornbread and showed it to Coates.

"Did you get anything?" he asked.

"A small slab of bacon," Coates replied.

"Good," said Foote. "Then I guess we're all set to go."

"Right. We'll leave at noon today."

For the rest of the morning, Foote paced nervously around the prison yard. He could hardly wait to make his break.

When the sun reached its peak in the sky, Foote knew the time had come. He took a deep breath and stood for a moment looking out across the prison yard. Then, with his heart pounding, he picked up his blanket. He wrapped it around his pipe, tobacco, and cornbread. He tucked the blanket under his arm and walked over to his friend.

"This is it," Coates whispered as they moved toward the edge of the prison yard. "This is our chance to escape."

Foote nodded. He and Coates had discussed their plan for days. Now he knew exactly what to do. Still, he felt his legs shaking as he stopped in front of the sentry on guard.

"The captain says we have to go into the woods to collect some fresh pine branches for bedding," Foote announced.

The sentry looked puzzled. "Right now?" he asked.

"Yup," said Coates. "He even made us bring our blankets to carry the branches back."

The young sentry paused for a minute. Then he shrugged. "Pass through," he said.

Slowly, Coates and Foote shuffled past him. They kept their eyes on the ground, pretending to resent this latest work assignment. When they were safely out of sight, they started to hurry. Soon they were running as fast as they could.

FOR hours they raced through the woods. Finally, at dusk, they stopped to rest.

"Now what?" Coates asked when he had caught his breath.

"Well," said Foote, "we've got to head southeast. We've got to find the Santee River and follow it all the way to the Atlantic Ocean. Once we're on the beach, we'll look for a Union gunboat that can pick us up."

"But the Atlantic is more than a hundred miles away. How are we going to make it that far without getting caught? Every step we take will be inside enemy territory."

"I don't know," said Foote quietly. "I'm not sure we can. But we've got to try."

The two men sat silently in the fading light, thinking over the dangers that lay ahead. Then, all of a sudden, they heard a distant whistling sound. As they listened, the sound grew louder.

"Dogs!" Foote cried in a frantic whisper. "They're after us with dogs!"

Picking up their blankets, Foote and Coates

took off through the woods. But the prison officials were gaining on them.

"Quick, go that way!" Foote cried, pointing to a
swamp. "They can't follow our scent through
water."

Moments later they were in the muddy swamp,
slogging through the water. Dead branches
caught their clothing. Soon their shirts were
ripped to rags and their arms were scratched and
bleeding. Still they kept plunging forward
through the cold, dark swamp. At last, the sound
of the dogs grew faint. Only then did the two fugitives stop running and crawl out of the swamp.

"Sounds like they've lost our trail," Coates said with relief.

"Yes," said Foote. "For now. But you can bet there'll be more dogs after us."

FOR the next few hours, the two men crept quietly through the woods. It was so dark they could barely see where they were going. At daybreak they found themselves in a clearing on the edge of a plantation. Looking across the field, they saw a black man with his back to them, chopping wood.

Coates looked blankly at Foote. "What should we do?" he whispered.

"I — I think we should ask him for help," Foote replied hesitantly.

"But what if he tells his master? What makes you think we can trust him?"

"I don't know if we can trust him or not. But we need to get directions, and I'd sooner ask him than his master."

Foote slowly stepped out of the woods and approached the man. Coates followed a few paces behind. When the slave saw them, he stopped swinging his ax and gave them a long, curious look.

"We're strangers around here and need some directions," said Foote.

"If I were you, I'd get some different clothes before I traveled much further in this county, mister," the slave replied.

Foote and Coates looked down at their prison clothes. Foote knew he had nothing to lose by telling the truth. "We're Union officers and we've just escaped from the prison camp. The guards and their dogs are after us … please — can you help us?"

The black man did not answer. He simply put down his ax and motioned for them to follow him. He led them to a thicket and pointed to a big hollow log.

"You hide in there till dark," he said. "I'll come back with some clothes and a canoe so you can ride down the Congaree River to the Santee."

Gratefully, Coates and Foote squirmed into the hollow log. As they lay there, however, doubts began to flood their minds.

"Suppose this is a trick?" Coates worried. "Suppose he's gone to get his master?"

Foote had no answer. He, too, felt nervous about trusting his life to a stranger.

WHEN evening came, the two men strained their ears, listening for the return of the woodcutter. At last they heard footsteps. Then a voice whispered for them to come out. Hesitantly, they backed out of the log. They were relieved to see their new friend. He gave them some sweet potatoes and old work clothes. Then he told them where they could find the canoe.

"Thank you," Foote said, shaking his hand. "We were afraid to trust you, but you've been a real friend."

The man brushed aside Foote's words. "When you need more help, just find the slave quarters. Tell them who you are. They'll help you. Every slave in the South is supporting the Union. Just don't forget us when you win the war. Come back and set us free."

"You can count on that," Foote promised. Then he and Coates took off through the woods toward the Congaree River and the canoe that was waiting for them.

For the next several days, Foote and Coates made progress down the river. They stayed close to the banks so they could scramble up into the woods if anyone approached. Every morning they stopped and went in search of a plantation. They got food, directions, and encouragement from the slaves they met. One old woman even had good news to tell them.

"Master Lincoln's been reelected," she announced. "And everyone around here thinks the North is going to win the war."

ABOUT a week later, Foote and Coates reached the Santee River. Here they stopped and went in search of more food. When they saw a black man working in a peanut patch, they motioned him over to the edge of the woods. Then they explained their situation and asked for help.

"Meet me tonight under that tree," he said, pointing to a large cottonwood.

All day Foote and Coates waited in the bushes. When night came, they approached the tree. Suddenly they heard dogs barking and saw men with torches running toward them.

"Oh, no!" cried Coates. "He's turned us in!"

Foote's stomach turned to knots. Was it possible? Had the man really betrayed them?

As Foote turned to run, he saw the black man trotting toward him. Then he realized that all the men carrying torches were black. So were those holding the dogs' leashes.

"What's going on?" he called out in confusion.

"Don't worry, nothing's wrong," the man said as he moved closer. "We needed an excuse to leave our cabins after dark. So I asked our master if a few of us could go possum hunting. We brought the dogs to make it look real."

Foote felt weak with relief as he heard these

words. After the man gave them food and information about the Santee River, Foote and Coates thanked him and headed back to the river.

It took another week for them to reach the Atlantic Ocean. To their delight, a Union gunboat was stationed right off the coast. Some gunners spotted them and sent a small boat over to pick them up. As Foote and Coates climbed aboard the ship, they raised their voices in a cheer for the Union.

Coates was sent to a hospital to recover from the ordeal, but Foote asked to be sent out to a fighting unit as soon as possible. More than ever before, he wanted to join the fight to help preserve the Union.

Now he had an additional reason for fighting. He wanted to help the slaves who had helped him. He wanted to win freedom for his newfound friends.

Philip Sheridan
A Leader for the North

"We must drive the Confederate army out of the Shenandoah Valley! They've been using it as a base to raid Northern cities. As long as they hold that valley, the North isn't safe. There's only one man who can drive the Confederates out of there. And that man is Philip Sheridan!"

S HERIDAN, I have a very important mission for you." General Grant spoke slowly, carefully. "I want you to take 10,000 cavalry troops to northern Virginia. There, you will have two assignments. Your first job is to drive all Confederate forces out of the Shenandoah Valley. We cannot allow them to continue their attacks from that area."

Sheridan knew that Southern General Jubal Early commanded the enemy forces in the valley. He also knew that Early was a bold and fearless

soldier. But Philip Sheridan was not afraid of any man. He accepted the challenge enthusiastically.

"Yes, sir," he said, "and what is the second assignment?"

"I want you to destroy everything in the valley — the fields, the crops, the cattle. Everything!"

Sheridan looked confused. He had not expected this task.

"Excuse me, sir," he said. "May I ask your reasons for this order?"

"Sheridan," General Grant said, "that valley is one of the most fertile areas in this country. Everything grows there. Over the last three years, it has supplied the Confederate army with provisions and shelter. As long as the Confederates have a good supply of food and a place to hide, they will never surrender. One way to bring this bloody war to a quicker end is to cut off their food supplies. A hungry army is a weak army."

Sheridan nodded. He didn't like the idea of destroying crops. But he understood why it had to be done.

"Yes, sir," he said. "I'll take care of it, sir."

So, in August 1864, Sheridan gathered his troops and led them to the Shenandoah Valley in northern Virginia. But instead of attacking immediately, he had his men set up camp.

"The time isn't right," he announced. "General Early has many more troops than we have. If we go charging in now, he'll overpower us. We'll wait until we have the advantage."

"When will that be?" asked one of Sheridan's advisers.

"I'm not sure," Sheridan responded. "But if we wait long enough, General Early will think we're afraid to attack. He'll decide he doesn't need as many troops to protect the valley. He'll send some men off to another war zone. And that's when we'll strike."

Sheridan's advisers shook their heads skeptically. But they followed orders and spread the word among the soldiers. There would be no attack until Sheridan ordered it.

For nearly six weeks, Sheridan and his men camped at the entrance of the valley. Meanwhile, other Union army officials began to grumble. In the North, newspapers ran headlines calling Phil Sheridan a coward and a failure. Even General Grant questioned his decision to wait.

None of this bothered Sheridan. He remained calm and confident.

"It doesn't matter what people think," he declared. "I've got a job to do, and I'm going to make sure it's done right."

AT last, on September 18, 1864, one of Sheridan's scouts dashed up to him.

"General! Your plan has worked. Early has just ordered half his troops to leave the valley!"

Sheridan smiled. "I knew it," he said under his breath. "I knew I could outsmart that Jubal Early."

That same day, Sheridan gave his men the order to march. All night they tramped through the woods. By morning, they met Early and his army just outside the town of Winchester, Virginia.

"All right, men," cried Sheridan, "this is it! This is what we've been waiting for! Begin the attack!"

With Sheridan leading the way, the Union soldiers charged toward the enemy. They sent out a fierce volley of bullets, shells, and cannonballs. The Confederates answered with firepower of their own. As the opposing lines drew closer, the noise became deafening. Smoke filled the air. The men couldn't see, couldn't hear, couldn't tell if they were winning or losing. Still they kept fighting. Every now and then, through the haze, they caught a glimpse of Sheridan leading the charge.

"Keep up the fight, men!" he cried. "Press forward, they'll run!"

The battle went on for hours. At last the Union troops broke through the Confederate ranks.

Immediately the Confederate soldiers panicked and retreated into the woods.

"Follow them!" cried Sheridan.

Sheridan's men obeyed his command. For two days and two nights they chased the enemy south through the valley. Finally, they reached Fisher's Hill. Here, Early and his men staked out a three-mile stretch just behind Tumbling River. The river kept the Confederates safe from a frontal attack. And jagged mountains on each side protected their flanks. There seemed to be no way Union forces could attack them.

SHERIDAN, however, was not ready to quit. Boldly he ordered his men to divide into three groups.

"When darkness comes, Company A will circle to the left, and Company B will circle to the right. I know it won't be easy, but we've got to reach those Confederates. Company C will stay here and prepare to attack from the front."

All night long the troops struggled to get into position to attack. Through sheer determination, they managed to get past all the barriers ... rocks, ledges, and the swirling river that blocked their way. By daybreak, they were set. When Sheridan sounded the call, they swooped down and attacked the surprised Confederate forces.

This attack caught Early's men completely by surprise. The Confederates, certain that their position was safe, hadn't even bothered to reload their weapons. At first, they tried bravely to hold off the swarms of Union troops. But soon they had to turn and run for their lives.

Once again Sheridan ordered his men to pursue the fleeing Confederate troops. During the next 24 hours, he and his men chased the Confederates right out of the valley. At last, Sheridan ordered his men to stop the chase.

"There!" he cried. "That will show them. Now Jubal Early and his troops are nothing but a memory in this valley!"

FOR the next ten days, Sheridan focused on his second mission — to destroy every agricultural resource in the valley.

"Level everything you see," Sheridan commanded his men. "Leave the people of this valley nothing to eat — no homes to live in — nothing."

He and his men burned farms, slaughtered animals, and trampled crops. In a few short days, they changed the Shenandoah Valley from an agricultural paradise to a blackened wasteland.

"Doesn't it bother you to destroy crops, and animals, and people's homes?" one soldier asked Sheridan.

"No," he responded. "I know how important the valley is to the Confederates, and I know it must be destroyed."

B Y mid-October, Sheridan had accomplished his objective. Leaving his troops at Cedar Creek, he made a quick trip to Washington to meet with General Grant. Grant was so pleased with Sheridan's work that he gave him a promotion and a one-hundred-gun salute.

On his way back to his troops, Sheridan spent the night in Winchester, Virginia. The next morning, October 20, Sheridan awoke to a distant, thundering sound.

"That's odd," he thought. "It sounds like cannonfire."

As he rode along the trail back to his camp at Cedar Creek, he spotted figures in the distance galloping toward him. As they came closer, he was shocked to see that they were his own troops. They were riding wildly, with a sickening look of fear on their faces.

"Early's come back!" one of them cried out to Sheridan. "He's got new troops, and he's come back for revenge!"

When Sheridan heard this, his eyes flashed with purpose and fury. Digging his spurs into his horse, he charged toward Cedar Creek, waving his hat and calling out to his retreating men.

"Turn back, men! Turn back! We're going to whip them out of their boots!"

The men gave a wild cheer of recognition. Inspired by Sheridan's courage, the retreating soldiers turned around and followed their leader back to Cedar Creek, cheering as they went.

When they reached the battlefield, the men stood their ground and fought with a new strength. Now that General Sheridan was leading them, they felt they could defeat any foe. After several hours of fighting, they turned back Early's army. Sheridan and his troops again had taken command of the Shenandoah Valley.

All across the North, citizens danced in the streets. Surely this defeat meant that the end was in sight! And, in less than six months, the dream came true. General Robert E. Lee surrendered to General Ulysses S. Grant at Appomattox Court House, Virginia. It was April 9, 1865. The bloody Civil War was finally over.

John Wilkes Booth

Actor Turned Assassin

For many years, I've been an actor. I've played many roles — heroes, villains, saints, and sinners. Now I am preparing to play my greatest role. I will be both actor and director. And my audience will be the entire world.

I will avenge the wrong that Lincoln has done to the South! This will be my most noble act!

PRESIDENT Abraham Lincoln stood at the White House window, watching a parade on Pennsylvania Avenue. He smiled as the sounds of the band floated in through the open window. His eyes sparkled with tears, and his whole face seemed lit with pride and relief.

"I have never been so happy in my life," the President whispered to his wife, Mary Todd Lincoln.

She squeezed his hand. It was April 14, 1865, and only five days ago General Robert E. Lee had surrendered to Union troops. The Civil War was over! The North had won!

The four years of war had taken a great toll on President Lincoln. His rugged face had grown old and haggard. His eyes had lost their shine. And his health had been weakened by the strain of war and the constant threats to his life. Now, at

last, he could relax — relax and enjoy the remainder of his second term as President of the United States.

He had no way of knowing that at that very moment, in a shabby boardinghouse across town, someone was plotting to end his life.

That someone was John Wilkes Booth. At the age of 26, Booth had already earned fame. He was considered one of the finest actors in the United States. Born and raised in Maryland, he had performed in both Northern and Southern states. He had recently finished a play at Ford's Theater in downtown Washington, D.C.

But behind the handsome face and riveting, coal-black eyes was a confused, troubled person. John Wilkes Booth was not just an actor. He was a man with a terrible plot. He was obsessed with one idea: the assassination of President Lincoln.

"The President must die," Booth told his friend, David Herold, again and again. "He alone is responsible for ruining this country. Because of him, a whole way of life has ended."

Herold, caught under Booth's power, merely nodded.

"It will be perfect, don't you see?" cried Booth. "I will destroy him, just as he destroyed the South."

Booth discussed his scheme with two other friends, Lewis Payne and George Atzerodt. Each time he spoke to them, they felt his power. His charm and the force of his convictions melted away all their objections. By April 14, they had agreed to help put his plan into action.

That morning, Booth stopped by Ford's Theater to pick up his mail. While talking to a stagehand, Booth learned that President and Mrs. Lincoln planned to attend the theater that evening to see the play, *Our American Cousin*.

"This is it," he whispered to himself. "This is the opportunity I've been waiting for."

Quickly Booth gathered his accomplices. He ordered Atzerodt to go to the Kirkwood Hotel and kill the Vice President. He ordered Payne and Herold to kill the Secretary of State at his home.

"And as for me," he announced with a crazed laugh, "I will kill the President! We will make the enemies of the Confederacy pay for what they've done."

ABOUT 9:30 that night, Booth appeared outside Ford's Theater. Dressed in a soft hat and high riding boots, he paced back and forth in front of the building. He entered the lobby several times. But each time he stopped at the door into the theater and walked back outside.

"Not yet," he thought to himself. "Not quite yet."

His heart thumped wildly, but he did not want to rush the deed. He knew the President and his wife would be sitting in special box seats overlooking the stage. He knew he could enter through a hallway behind the President's box and surprise him. He would wait for the perfect moment.

Finally, at 10:15, he decided the time had come. Humming under his breath, he walked into the theater and up the stairs. He walked quietly down the narrow hall.

Luck was with Booth. The special guard assigned to protect the President was not at his usual place outside the door of the box. Instead, he had taken a break and was away from his post.

Silently Booth looked through the peephole in the door. Right in front of him sat President Abraham Lincoln, his back to him. With a flourish, Booth drew his pistol and flung open the door. Aiming directly at the President, he pulled the trigger.

Instantly, Booth moved to the edge of the box and lunged over the railing, intending to take the stage and make a speech of triumph. Instead, the spur on his boot caught on the flag draped over the banister, and Booth fell to the stage twelve feet below, shattering a bone in his left leg.

But he was undaunted. Pulling out a knife and brandishing it wildly, he exclaimed: "Sic semper tyrannis!" — "Thus always for tyrants!"

As several men ran after him, he quickly hobbled to the back door. Once outside, he jumped on his waiting horse. Then, with one last triumphant laugh, he rode off into the night.

"I've done it!" he thought victoriously as he galloped toward the southwest. "Soon the whole country will know I have shot the President!"

AS he crossed the Navy Yard Bridge, he saw David Herold riding toward him in a panic.

"Well?" called Booth, stopping and speaking in a loud whisper. "Did you get the Secretary?"

Herold stammered. "Ahh — ahh — well, no, not really."

In truth, Herold had lost his nerve and fled the scene even before Payne, his accomplice, stabbed the Secretary. As it turned out, Payne had not carried out Booth's orders, either. He had wounded the Secretary, but had not killed him.

At that moment, however, none of this mattered to John Wilkes Booth. He felt delirious with excitement. After years of watching Lincoln's army destroy the South, he had finally taken revenge. He motioned for Herold to follow him. Then he spurred his horse back to a full gallop and rode off.

After an hour of riding, Booth's happiness began to fade. In its place came exhaustion, and the constant throbbing pain of his broken ankle.

"I must stop," he called to Herold. "I must get help for this ankle. Let's head for Dr. Mudd's."

Dr. Samuel Mudd, who had supported the South in the war, welcomed the two fugitives into his house. He gave them food and drink and tried to patch up Booth's leg.

"You should stay here until the ankle heals," he advised.

"No," said Booth, putting on his best theatrical voice, "we must ride on. We cannot rest until we are safely in the South."

F OR the next 24 hours, Booth and Herold rode fast and hard. Booth, although in great pain from his ankle, forced himself to keep going. Finally, on the morning of April 16, he and Herold reached the Potomac River. Here they met a friend named Thomas Jones, who lived on a nearby farm.

"This place is swarming with Union troops," Jones cautioned them. "So you'd better stay out of sight for a while."

Jones led them to a hiding place deep in a pine thicket. They stayed there for the next six days. Almost every hour they heard the cries of Union soldiers, the blare of bugles, or the stamping of horses' hooves. But they saw no one except Jones, who came every day to bring them food and newspapers.

Scanning the newspapers, Booth chuckled to himself.

"Look at this, Herold," he whispered gleefully. "Lincoln died at 7:00 A.M on April 15. He never even regained consciousness! Now everyone knows my name. I, John Wilkes Booth, assassinated Lincoln. I am famous!"

ON April 22, Jones ferried the two men across the Potomac River in a flatboat. From there, they traveled quickly through the Virginia countryside. After two more days of riding, Booth needed to rest again. His ankle was puffy and swollen, and he winced in pain as he tried to stay in the saddle. And so, on the afternoon of April 24, he and Herold stopped at the farm of Richard H. Garrett.

Booth told Garrett that he was a wounded Confederate soldier on his way home to Maryland. Garrett let Booth and Herold stay on his farm. The first night they slept in the main house. By the second night, Booth had become jumpy.

"I have a feeling the soldiers are closing in on us," he told Herold. "We'd better sleep in the tobacco barn tonight. That way we can get out of here first thing tomorrow morning."

At 3:00 A.M., Booth gave Herold a sharp nudge.

"Hey!" he hissed. "I think I hear something."

Looking out, they saw Union troops surrounding the barn. Immediately Herold hurried for the door.

"What are you doing?" Booth screamed.

"I surrender! I surrender!" cried Herold, running out into the custody of the soldiers.

Booth kicked the dirt floor in disgust.

When the soldiers called for his surrender, he shouted, "I will not be taken alive!"

Upon hearing this, a soldier ran around to the back of the barn. He tossed a lit match in through the open door. The fire ignited some dry hay, and instantly the building turned into walls of flames. Booth scrambled for the front door, brandishing a rifle in one hand and a pistol in the other. But he never fired either weapon. A single gunshot rang out from a soldier in the shadows. Booth fell to the ground.

As the nation mourned the death of the President, people were shocked and confused by the actions of Booth. His place in history was assured: not as a great actor or patriot, but as the man who killed President Abraham Lincoln.

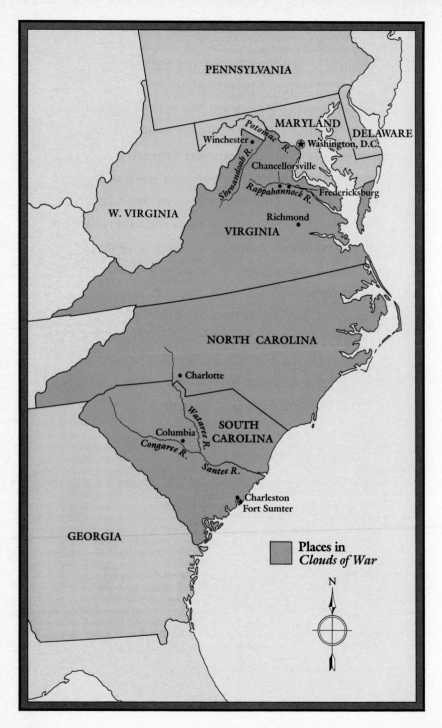